SUPERIFIC SCIENCE
MARINE BIOLOGY

by
LORRAINE CONWAY

illustrated by Linda Akins

Cover design by Nancee Volpe

GOOD APPLE, INC.
BOX 299
CARTHAGE, IL 62321-0299

5489

GOOD APPLE, INC.
BOX 299
CARTHAGE, IL 62321-0299

INTRODUCTION

Most students have a natural curiosity about the plant and animal life residing in the oceans and are eager to increase their knowledge in this area of study which has been neglected for years. With this growing interest in mind, *Marine Biology* has been written. The first step to learning about sea life is an acquisition of basic knowledge which can later be applied to areas of greater depth. By using simplified principles and concepts and putting them into various forms and approaches, this book hopes to give students a broad base on which to build and at the same time to arouse curiosity, build confidence, attain skills, and promote knowledge of this modern science.

TABLE OF CONTENTS

DIATOMS

Diatoms are microscopic plants which belong to a larger group of plants called algae. They consist of only one cell and are found in both fresh and salt water. Some diatoms are single forms while others group into chains. Most diatoms float with the current; others propel themselves with a jerk-like movement. All diatoms are made similarly in structure. They are composed of two almost equal halves. The slightly smaller of the halves fits into the other as in the side of a pillbox. Their cell walls are made of silica and form a glass-like shell which is often very beautiful.

The importance of diatoms as plankton and as a basic part of the food chain cannot be underestimated; they are a necessary food source for many small sea animals which are in turn eaten by larger forms. Without diatoms, most of the fish of the world could not exist.

The shells of diatoms do not dissolve in water. After the plant dies these shells sink to the bottom to become diatomaceous earth (diatomite). Diatomaceous earth is used extensively in industry as a filter, insulator, polisher, and extender in paint, brick, and tile.

Diatoms can be ordered live or in slides for microscopic study from biological supply houses. Diatomaceous earth can also be ordered very cheaply in powder form.

MAGIC SQUARE QUIZ ON DIATOMS

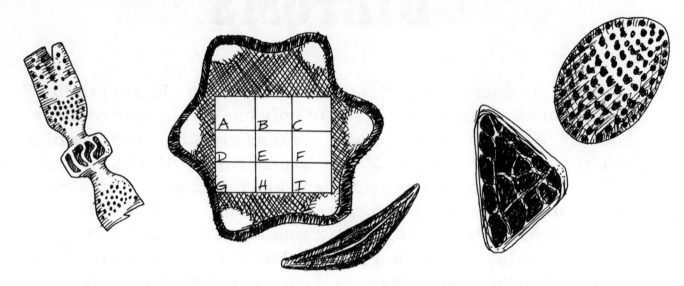

1. algae
2. pillbox
3. food chain

4. diatomite
5. silica
6. microscopic

7. diatomaceous earth
8. filter
9. small sea animals

Find the numbers of the answers for the lettered questions below. Put the numbers in the corresponding squares. If the answers are correct, each row of numbers will add up to the same total.

A. another name for diatomaceous earth
B. consume diatoms
C. the type of structure which all diatoms have
D. is the passing of food energy from one living thing to another
E. makes up the glassy cell wall of all diatoms
F. a name for the remains of dead diatoms
G. a use for diatoms in industry
H. the group of plants to which diatoms belong
 I. the size of diatoms

THE LIFE CYCLE OF THE JELLYFISH OBELIA

Cycle means circle. In this exercise you will put the various stages in the life cycle of a common jellyfish, Obelia, in a circle by following the instructions.

Cut out the six pieces on page 5. You will use the pieces to form a clocklike circle. Begin at twelve o'clock with the piece described in number one. Continue with the second description, which you will put in the two o'clock position. Continue until the life cycle (circle) of Obelia is complete.

In the life cycle of Obelia, it is important to remember that the offspring do not resemble their parents but are identical to their grandparents. This phenomenon is called alternation of generations.

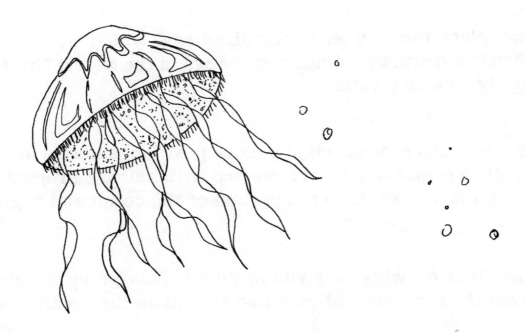

THE LIFE CYCLE OF THE JELLYFISH OBELIA

1. The polyp. This part of the life cycle is a stalk which resembles a leafless plant. On it are two different branches; one has tentacles or arms around the top surrounding the mouth. This is the feeding branch. It gets the food, digests it, and circulates it throughout the plant. The other branch, the reproductive branch, contains buds. The buds will ripen into free-swimming jellyfish. The piece matching this description goes into the 12 o'clock position.

2. At the two o'clock position, place the drawing of two free-swimming jellyfish. One of these is a male whose reproductive organs or testis will produce sperm. The other is a female whose ovaries produce eggs.

3. At four o'clock the drawing shows the egg and the sperm which have been released into the water by the free-swimming jellyfish.

4. Next place the zygote, or fertilized egg, which was formed when the sperm by chance met the egg in the water. This is in the six o'clock position.

5. The next piece, or the eight o'clock position, shows a larva, a small free-swimming form covered with hairlike projections. The larva will settle to the bottom of the ocean and begin to grow.

6. The final drawing is a young polyp. This polyp developed from the larva soon after it had settled on the ocean's floor.

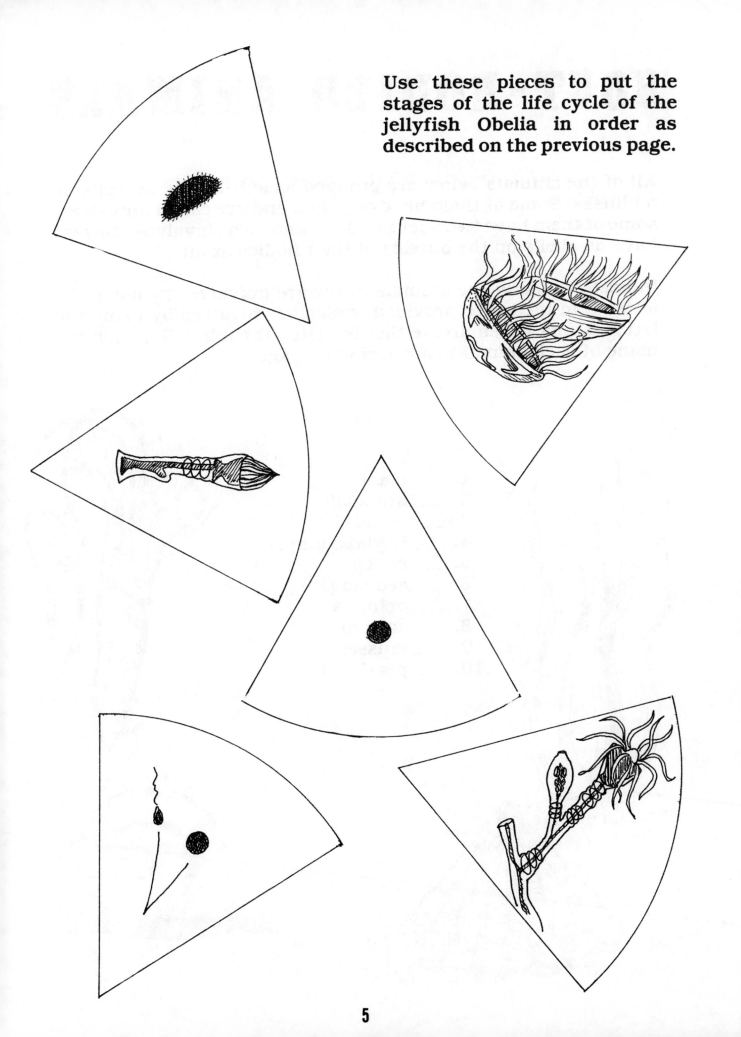

Use these pieces to put the stages of the life cycle of the jellyfish Obelia in order as described on the previous page.

SOFT-BODIED ANIMALS

All of the animals below are grouped as soft-bodied animals or mollusks. Some of them have one shell and are called univalves; some of them have two shells and are known as bivalves; the rest have no shells on the outside of their bodies at all.

Indicate which of the animals below are univalves by using the letter U in the space provided, which are bivalves by using the letter B, and which are neither by using the letter N. Match the name of each animal to a drawing on page 7.

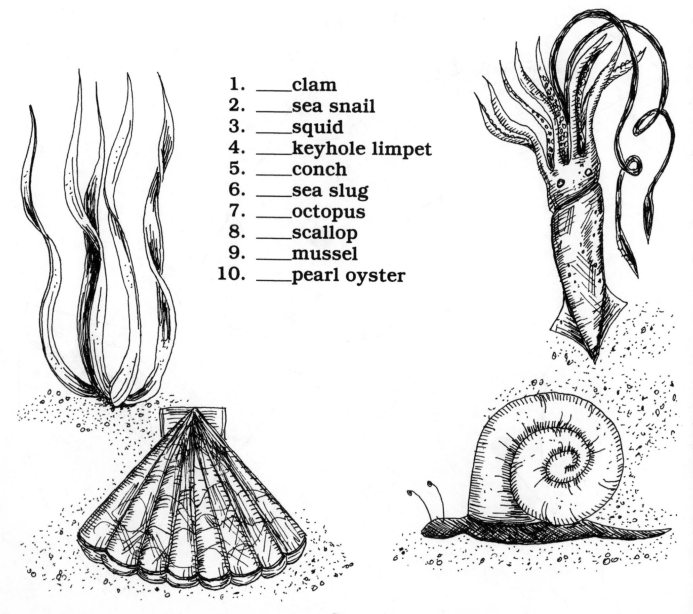

1. ____clam
2. ____sea snail
3. ____squid
4. ____keyhole limpet
5. ____conch
6. ____sea slug
7. ____octopus
8. ____scallop
9. ____mussel
10. ____pearl oyster

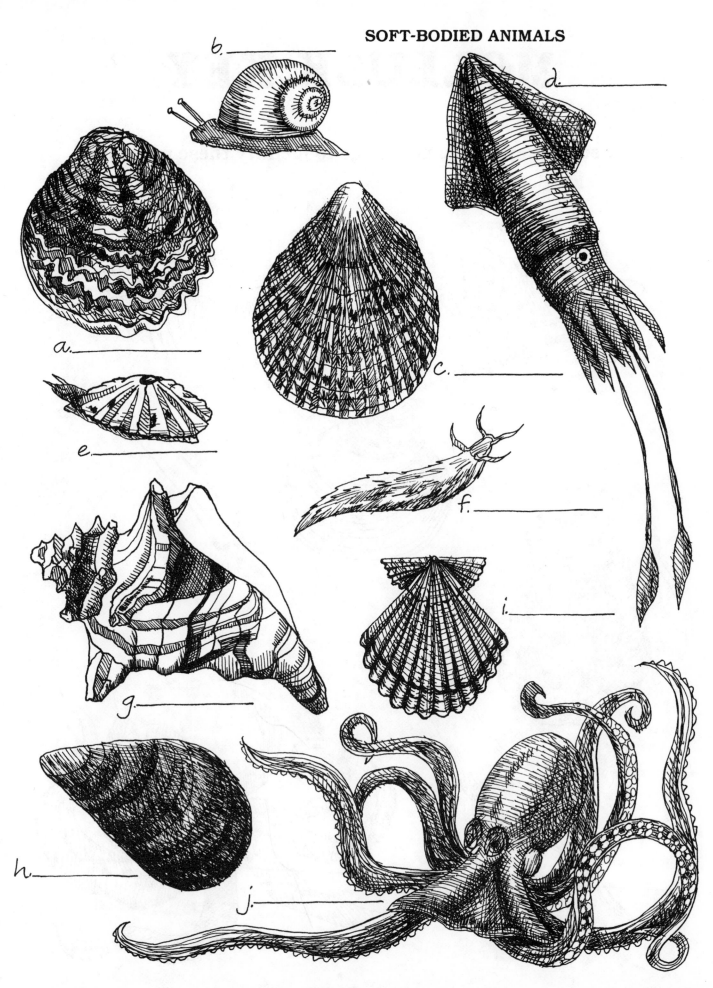

b._____

d._____

a._____

c._____

e._____

f._____

g._____

i._____

h._____

j._____

7

MOLLUSK KEY

Use the key on the next page to identify these mollusks.

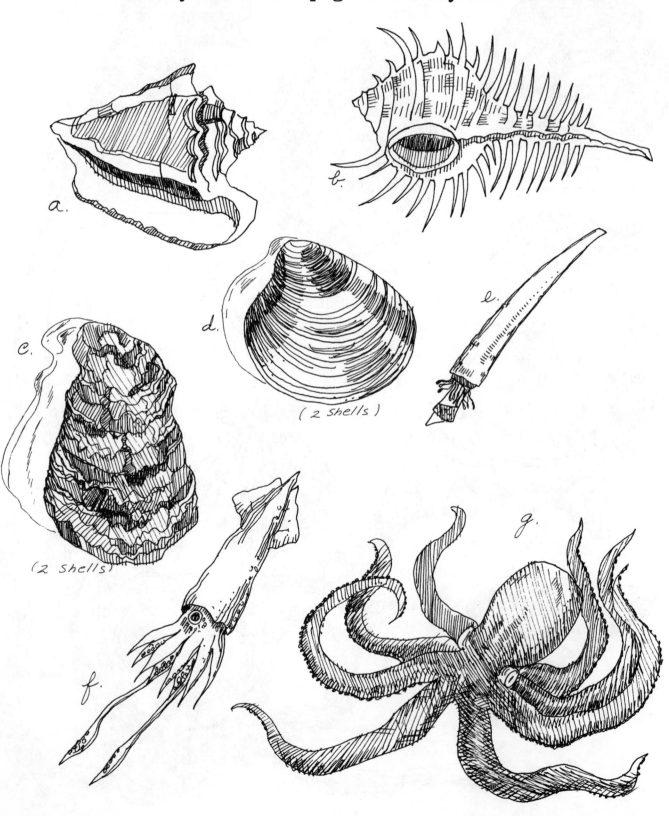

a.

b.

c.

(2 shells)

d.

(2 shells)

e.

f.

g.

MOLLUSK KEY

Keys are used by scientists to identify organisms which are not readily known. In order to use a key the student takes all the information he is given about an organism and follows the given steps exactly as indicated. Always start each organism at 1A, determine whether the description 1A or 1B fits, then follow the key as directed until the organism's name is reached at the end of the line.

1A	Soft body enclosed within a shell	See 2
1B	Soft body not covered by a shell	See 3
2A	Shell long and curved as an elephant's tusk	Tusk Shell
2B	Shell not long and curved	See 4A
3A	Body without outside shell and having eight arms.	Octopus
3B	Body without an outside shell and having ten arms, two longer than the others	Squid
4A	Body covered by one shell	See 5
4B	Body covered by two shells	See 6
5A	Shell covered with long spines	Spiny Murex
5B	Shell without long spines	Queen Conch
6A	Shell smooth with many even concentric growth lines	Clam
6B	Shell bumpy and uneven	Oyster

OCTOPUS OR SQUID?

Using the drawings below, compare the features of an octopus and a squid by indicating in the spaces below whether the given feature fits the octopus (O), squid (S), or both (B).

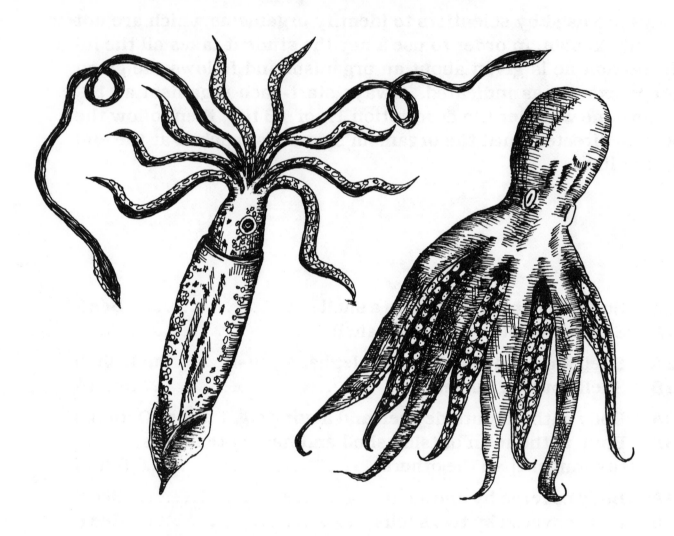

1. _____ eight arms, all similar in size.
2. _____ streamlined, pencil-shaped body.
3. _____ most arms have two rows of suckers.
4. _____ fins attached to body.
5. _____ body thick and rounded.
6. _____ ten arms, two longer than the others.
7. _____ body without fins.
8. _____ body is soft.
9. _____ well-developed eyes present.
10. _____ ocean dweller.

NAMES THAT FIT

Below are drawings of the shells of mollusks whose names aptly describe their appearances. See how many names you can match to the drawings.

razor clam   thorny oyster   worm shell   cone shell
tulip shell   sundial   ear shell   keyhole limpet
olive shell   turkey wing   bleeding tooth   angel's wing

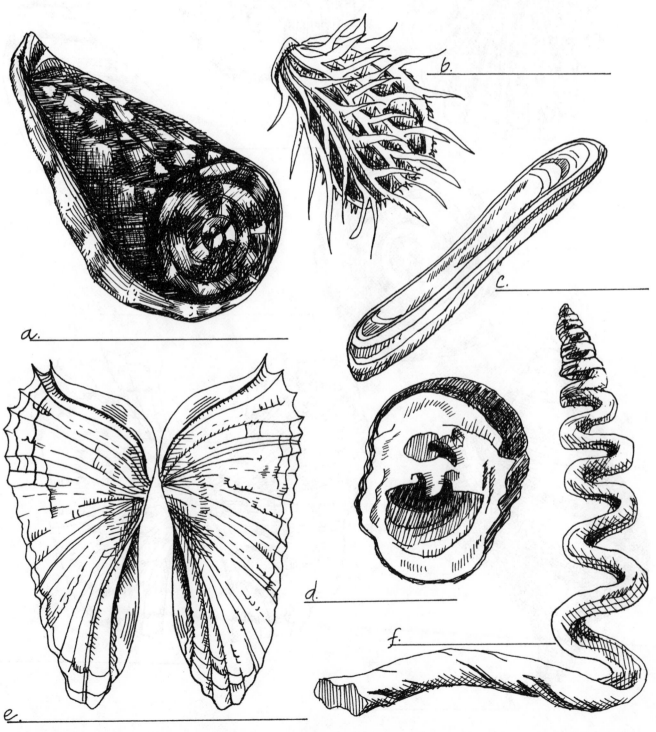

a. _____

b. _____

c. _____

d. _____

e. _____

f. _____

11

g. _____

h. _____

i. _____

j. _____

k. _____

l. _____

12

DIGESTIVE SYSTEMS
IN MOLLUSKS

Clams, snails, and squids all belong to the group of animals called Mollusks. Clams, oysters, scallops, mussels and their relatives belong to a special class of Mollusks called Pelecypoda (hatchet foot); snails, whelks, conchs and slugs belong to the class Gastropoda (stomach foot); and the squids, octopi, cuttlefish and nautilus belong to the class Cephalopoda (head foot). The three classes differ in structure and in the number or the presence or absence of shells but all have similar digestive systems. In the drawings below identify the animals and label the mouth, stomach, intestine, and anus in each. Color the digestive tract for each animal and fill in the chart at the bottom of the page.

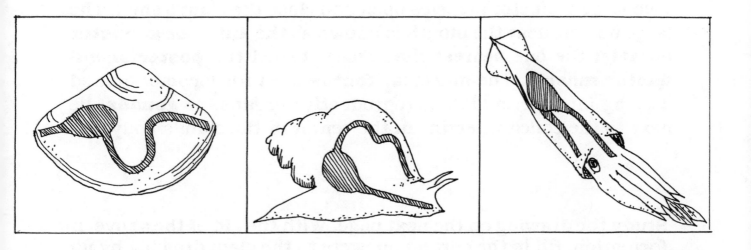

INTESTINAL PART	FUNCTION
Mouth	
Stomach	
Intestine	
Anus	

CLAMS

Clams are invertebrate (no backbone) animals belonging to a group called mollusks. They are closely related to oysters, scallops and other mollusks having two shells. The shells of a clam are hinged together at the back by an elastic ligament. The oldest part of the shell is the hump near the hinge. This hump is called the umbo. As the clam grows the **mantle,** which is the inside covering of the clam, secretes new layers of shell. Each line on the shell of the clam represents a layer of growth.

Water enters the clam by means of an **incurrent siphon** bringing with it food and oxygen. The food is taken in at the **mouth**; from there it passes into the stomach which leads to the coiled **intestine.** Waste is excreted at the end of the intestine at an opening called the **anus.** Water which has circulated inside the clam shell carries the waste out through the **excurrent siphon.** Two large adductor muscles open and close the clam's shell. The large muscle near the mouth is known as the **anterior adductor muscle;** the one nearest the anus is called the **posterior adductor muscle.** The muscular **foot** is used for locomotion and digging into the mud. The reproductive organs, or **gonads,** lie next to the coiled intestine in the center of the clam's body.

Study the drawing on the next page. With the aid of the above information, fill in the correct answers to the clam drawing by using the bold words to name the parts of the clam's anatomy.

Clam

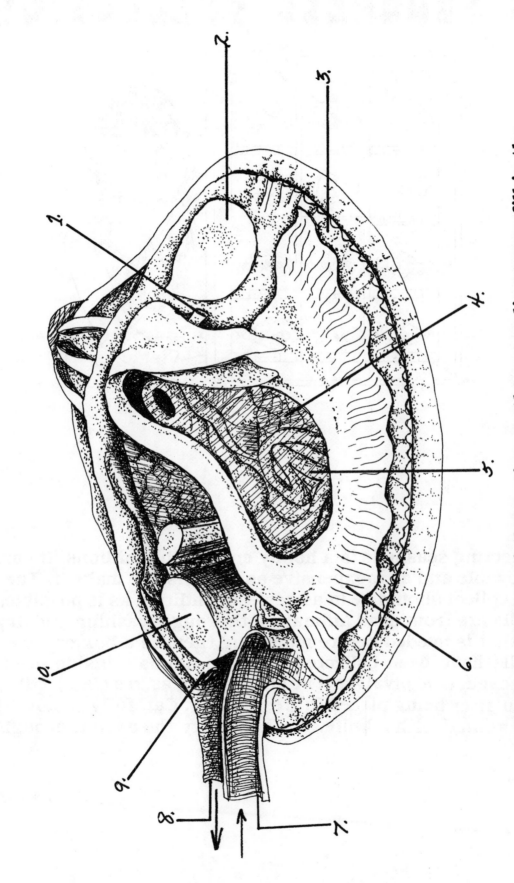

With the aid of the information on the preceding page, fill in the correct answers to the clam drawing by using the bold words to name the parts of the clam's anatomy.

A SEASHELL COLLECTION

Collecting seashells is a hobby enjoyed by millions. It can be as enjoyable and as inexpensive as you wish to make it. The shells you collect should be in as perfect condition as is possible. If the shells are from dead animals, a thorough washing and drying is all that is needed before mounting them in a box or case. If the shells have been collected live, the animals inside need to be removed. Live bivalves (two shells, such as in a clam) will usually open after being placed in fresh water. Carefully remove the entire animal with a knife. Wash and dry the shell thoroughly.

Live univalves (one shell, such as in a snail) need to be placed in boiling water for one or two minutes. The animal inside can be pulled out with a coat hanger or wire. Clean the shell thoroughly. Some shells have a covering or door to the inside of the shell called an operculum. The operculum is valuable to your collection. Remove it carefully and clean it of all flesh by gently scraping it with a knife. After the animal has been removed and the shell cleaned, glue the operculum to a piece of cotton and place in its orginal position.

**Strombus alatus
Sanibel Island, Florida
June 10, 1980
Sean Conway**

To make your shells shiny, polish them with a little mineral oil and a soft cloth. Display your shells on a bookcase, shelf, or in a case or box. Use a reference book to identify your shells with their scientific names. The scientific name of an organism has two parts written in Latin. The first word is a noun and is capitalized. The second word is an adjective and describes the organism. The second word is never capitalized. The other information you will need in addition to the name of the shell is the place and date where the shell was obtained. The collector's name is written on the bottom of the card. The card is placed beneath the shell in the case or box. If the shells are kept on a shelf, keep a file of your shells.

The Oyster Mystery

"Another poor catch," Captain Williams complained to the men aboard the fishing trawler, **Pearl.** "It's getting worse and worse every year; soon we'll all be landlubbers, like it or not."

"Getting so no man can make a living dragging for oysters anymore," responded the first mate, Mr. Wren.

"If only there weren't so many starfish." There was now anger in the captain's voice. "Seems they are increasing at the same rate the oysters are decreasing."

"What can we do?" Mr. Wren continued as he sorrowfully studied the nets full of empty oyster shells and fat, crawling starfish.

"We can't go on this way; the only sensible thing left to do is throw back any live oysters - give them a chance to grow and reproduce while we destroy the starfish we catch. It's our last chance to save the oyster industry," the captain finished the conversation.

At Captain William's request the Oysterman's Association met and decided to heed his advice. Next season they would reverse their usual procedure by keeping the starfish and returning the oysters to the sea. The question now came up of what to do with the tons of live starfish caught in the nets. They discussed many plans. Bury the starfish was one suggestion; but that was too much trouble and would take too long. Beach them was another suggestion but that would create a mess and disfigure the beaches. Someone must have a better idea. "I've got it!" Mr. Wren shouted gleefully. "We know we can't just throw them back into the water to be pulled up again, so let's destroy them by chopping them into pieces on deck and sweeping them back into the sea." A fine suggestion, they all agreed.

Two years later the oyster fishermen were very excited about the prospect of an enormous catch. Their disappointment came early. When the nets were pulled from the sea there were more starfish than any of them had ever seen in a lifetime. What did the oyster fishermen do wrong? Can you solve the oyster mystery?

MISNOMERS OF THE SEA

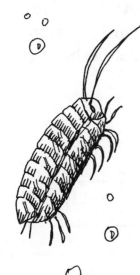

A misnomer is the use of a wrong name. Misnomers are often applied to plants or animals to show a resemblance to another or different kind of plant, animal or object.

EXAMPLE: Sand dollar is a misnomer because it is neither made of sand nor is it a dollar; it is a spiny-skinned animal which lives in ocean sand.

The sea organisms on the next page are obviously not what their names indicate them to be. In the space provided, tell why they are misnomers.

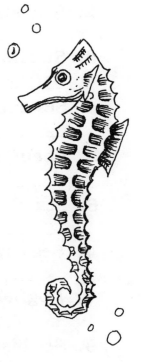

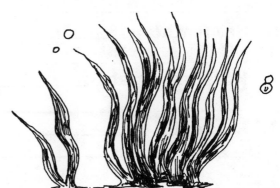

MISNOMERS OF THE SEA

The animals below are not really what their names tell us they are. Write in the spaces provided the reasons they are misnamed. If you do not know, consult a good resource or reference book.

1. Jellyfish _____
   _____

2. Sea horse _____
   _____

3. Starfish _____
   _____

4. Sea cucumber _____
   _____

5. Shellfish _____
   _____

6. Sea lily _____
   _____

7. Sea cow _____
   _____

8. Dogfish _____
   _____

9. Sea biscuit _____
   _____

10. Sea feather _____
    _____

11. Horseshoe crab _____
    _____

12. Sea robin _____
    _____

ECHINODERMATA
(spiny - skinned animals)

The members of this group of animals are called Echinodermata because of their spiny skins. The word Echinodermata comes from two Greek words, echinos meaning hedgehog, an unusual animal with sharp spines, and dermis, which means skin. Another feature of this group of animals is their symmetry. Echinodermata are radially symmetrical; that is, they have no head or tail ends. Their bodies are built on a circular or radial plan with their mouths located in the center.

Spiny-skinned animals are known for their powers of regeneration, or the regrowing of lost parts. This is especially true of the starfish and brittle stars. A single arm or ray with a portion of the center will regenerate into a complete organism.

On the next page are five types of Echinodermata. Match the drawings to their names; the brief descriptions at the bottom of this page will help you.

1. The sea urchin has been described as a walking pincushion.
2. The sea cucumber somewhat resembles a cucumber in shape.
3. A brittle star's or serpent star's arms often break off because of their length and brittleness.
4. A sea lily remotely resembles a plant, which, of course, it isn't.
5. Named for its shape, just about everyone recognizes the common starfish.

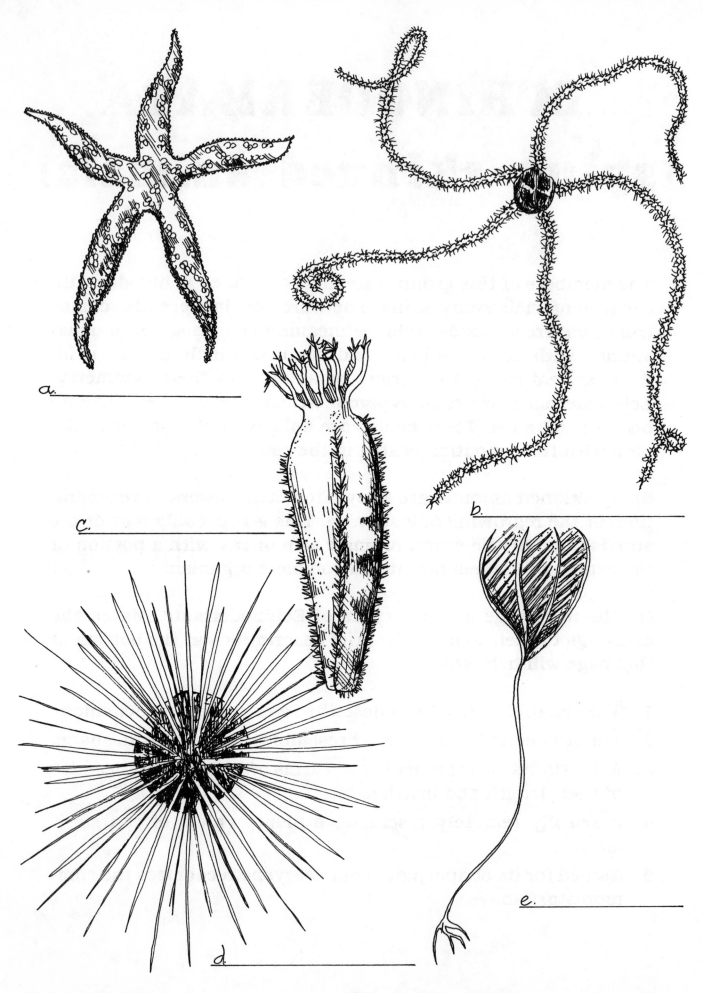

a. _____

b. _____

c. _____

d. _____

e. _____

STARFISH

What animals do you think of when the word "seashore" is mentioned? If starfish come to mind, you think as many others do. Starfish are common seashore animals often washed ashore by storms and tides. They belong to an unusual group of animals known to scientists as the Echinodermata, or spiny-skinned animals.

There are over 1700 different kinds of starfish and in their natural surroundings they are arrayed in glorious colors such as orange, pink, red, purple, blue, green and brown. They walk on their five rays by means of a special and complicated canal system which pumps water into the hundreds of tube feet located on the underside of their bodies. The pressure of the water in the tube feet causes them to expand, then contract, exerting suction against the surface on which the starfish is walking. This suction enables the starfish to open the shells of clams and oysters, its favorite foods. The mouth of the starfish is centered on the underside of the body, allowing it to swallow a mollusk easily once the shell has been pried open.

Starfish do not have well-developed sense organs, but they do have a simple nervous system. From a nerve ring around its mouth, a nerve extends out to the tip of each ray and ends in a light-sensitive eyespot. It is believed that the eyespot permits the starfish to detect changes in the environment.

STARFISH

How many of these questions can you answer? Refer to page 23 if necessary.

1. To which group of animals do starfish belong?
2. What does this group word mean?
3. What are some of the colors of live starfish?
4. Where is the mouth of a starfish located?
5. What are two uses of tube feet?
6. What are the sense organs of starfish called?
7. What are the two uses of these sense organs?
8. How many different kinds of starfish are there?
9. What do starfish eat?
10. How do starfish walk?
11. What one word describes the nervous system of starfish?
12. In what environment would you find starfish?

STARFISH

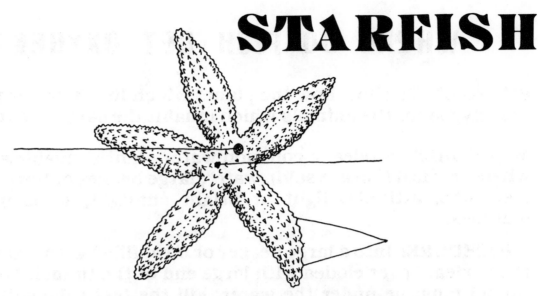

TOPSIDE OR ABORAL SURFACE

On the above drawing of the starfish, label the large sieve plate, which brings water into the canal system; the anus, where wastes are excreted; and the spines, which are part of the skeletal system.

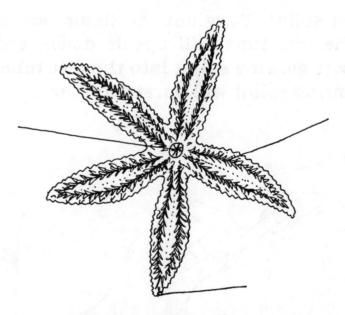

UNDERSIDE OR ORAL SURFACE

Label the mouth which lies in the center of the oral side, the many tube feet which propel the starfish, and the light-sensitive eyespots.

WHERE DO FISH GET OXYGEN?

PURPOSE: To show how the plants which live in water produce the oxygen for the animals which inhabit the same environment.

MATERIALS: Elodea (a common water plant available at stores where tropical fish are sold), water, large beaker or bowl, funnel, test tube, artificial light or bright sunlight, wooden splint, matches.

PROCEDURE: Into a large beaker or bowl filled with water, place the elodea. Cover elodea with large end of the funnel. Top of the funnel must be under the water. Fill the test tube with water. With thumb securely over the test tube, invert it and place over the funnel. DO NOT ALLOW AIR TO ENTER THE TEST TUBE. Place in bright light for several hours. Lift test tube carefully. If there is a little water left in the test tube, allow it to drain quickly while still upside down. When the water has drained, place thumb again over the mouth of the test tube.

Light a wooden splint. Blow out the flame, leaving a glowing splint. With the test tube still upside down, quickly remove thumb and insert glowing splint into the test tube. If oxygen is present the glowing splint will burst into flame.

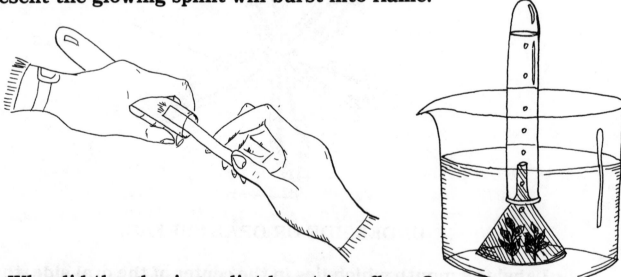

1. Why did the glowing splint burst into flame?
2. What produced the oxygen?
3. Describe how the oxygen replaced the water in the test tube.
4. What meaning does this experiment have to oceanic plants and animals?

A LITTLE ECOSYSTEM
OF YOUR OWN

Most bodies of water such as lakes, ponds and oceans are balanced by nature with the plants and animals which have lived there for long periods of time; they are self-sufficient environments or ecosystems. Each living thing in an ecosystem has a particular job to do in order to help keep that balance. Most of the aquaria you have seen are not truly balanced because air and food have been added. To make an ecosystem of your own in which you will not need to add food or air, follow the instructions below.

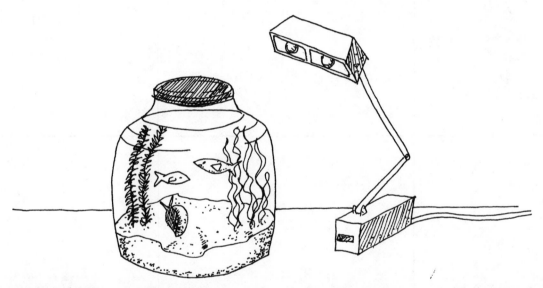

PURPOSE: To learn the value of ecosystems and to understand their basic functions.

MATERIALS: A small fish, one or two inches long; two or three freshwater snails, a variety of freshwater aquatic plants, large (two-gallon) jar with cap and wide mouth, clean, coarse sand or fine gravel, water.

PROCEDURE: Thoroughly wash sand and place in bottom of jar. Fill the jar with water and allow to stand 2 days before adding fish and snails. Anchor plants in sand and cover. Place in good light but out of direct sun (a lamp with a 75 watt bulb can be used). Regulate light as needed. If plants begin to lose their color, give them more light.

ORGANISM	WHAT IT GIVES TO THE ECOSYSTEM	WHAT IT TAKES FROM THE ECOSYSTEM

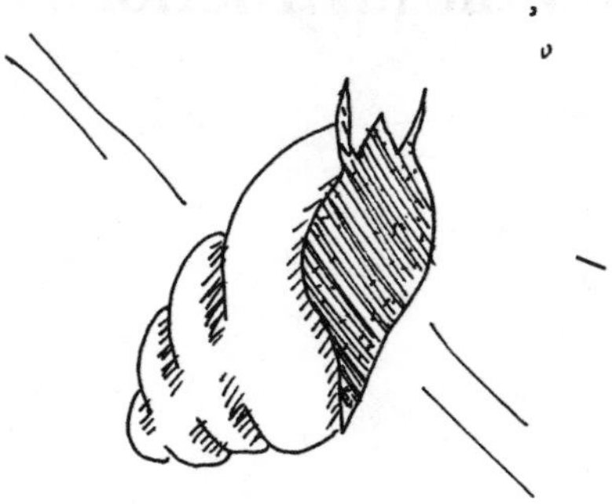		

1. Fill in the above chart.
2. Why did you allow the water to stand before adding the living material?
3. Could the ecosystem survive without light? Why or why not?
4. Describe what happens when an ecosystem becomes imbalanced.

RESPIRATION RATE OF GOLDFISH

PURPOSE: To determine whether or not the temperature of water has an effect on the breathing rate of goldfish.

MATERIALS: Three goldfish, three large beakers or jars, ice, hot water, fishnet, clock or watch, centigrade thermometer.

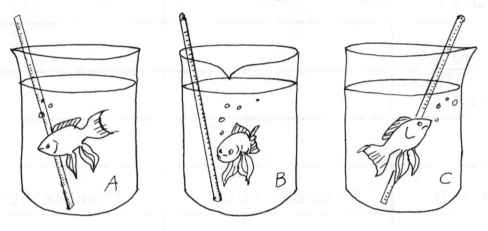

PROCEDURE: Place each fish in a separate beaker or jar which has been filled with water at room temperature. (If tap water is being used, it should have been set out the day before.) Label the beakers A, B, and C and place a thermometer in each. Time the breathing rate of each fish by counting the opening and closing of its gill covers for one minute. Record as trial 1 for fish A, B, and C on tables on the next page. Slowly add ice to jar A until the temperature falls 5° C. Record the respiration rate of the goldfish after counting for one minute. Add more ice until the temperature drops another 5° C. Check and record the respiration rate. To beaker B add hot water very *slowly* (do not add the hot water directly over the fish) until the temperature rises 5° C.

Check and record the respiration rate. Continue to add the hot water until the temperature rises another 5° centigrade. Record data. Beaker C is the control; do not add anything to it. Take two additional one-minute readings of the respiration rate of the goldfish in beaker C. Record. Allow the water in beakers A and B to return to normal room temperature. Then place the fish in a well aerated container.

FISH A	TEMPERATURE	RESPIRATION
Trial 1		
Trial 2		
Trial 3		

FISH B	TEMPERATURE	RESPIRATION
Trial 1		
Trial 2		
Trial 3		

FISH C	TEMPERATURE	RESPIRATION
Trial 1		
Trial 2		
Trial 3		

1. Describe what happened to goldfish A as the water temperature dropped.

2. Describe goldfish B as the water temperature rose.

3. Describe the activities of goldfish C.

4. Which goldfish, A or B, better tolerated the experiment?

5. Do you think goldfish B could withstand a further rise in temperature? Why or why not?

6. What do you think might happen to the fish if the ice and hot water were added all at once to fish A and fish B?

7. What factors other than temperature could influence the breathing rates of fish?

8. Why did you allow the goldfish to return slowly to normal water temperatures?

9. You may wish to use your data from the tables to construct a bar or line graph showing the relationship between water temperatures and respiration rates of goldfish.

SPELLING NAMES OF FISH

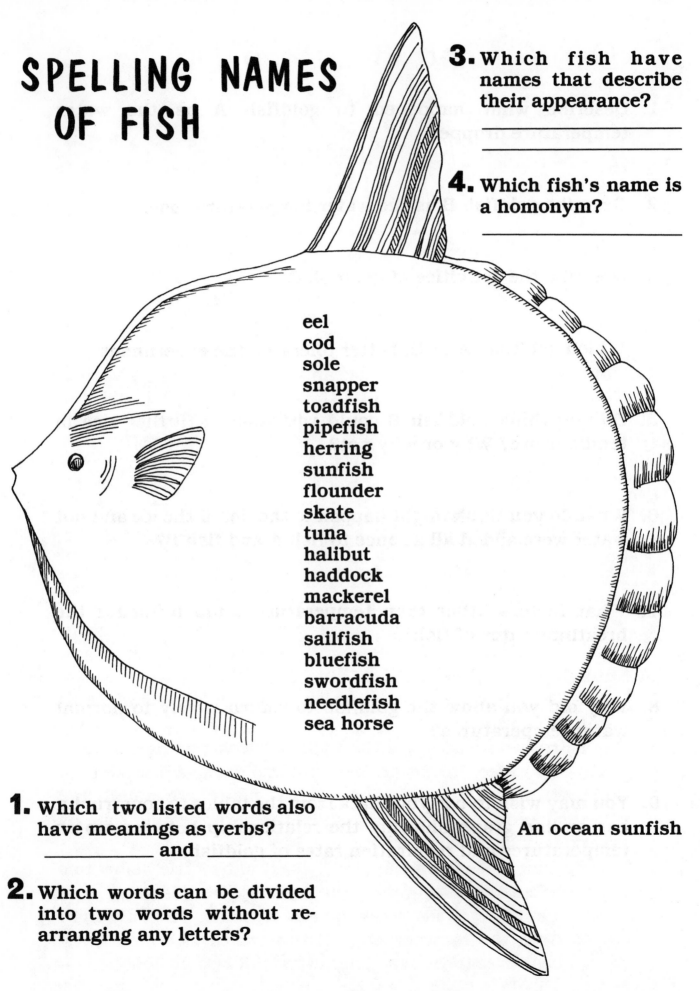

3. Which fish have names that describe their appearance?
_____
_____

4. Which fish's name is a homonym?
_____

eel
cod
sole
snapper
toadfish
pipefish
herring
sunfish
flounder
skate
tuna
halibut
haddock
mackerel
barracuda
sailfish
bluefish
swordfish
needlefish
sea horse

1. Which two listed words also have meanings as verbs?
_____ and _____

2. Which words can be divided into two words without re-arranging any letters?

An ocean sunfish

Depth Chart of Ocean Dwellers

Cut out the four pictures of ocean dwellers living at various depths on page 34. After reading the descriptions below, decide which picture is being described and attach the pictures in order from the surface dwelling animals to those inhabiting the great depths or abyss by using tape or paste. When finishing you will have a depth chart for ocean dwellers which looks like this:

1. The first picture which you will put at the top is of ocean surface dwellers and those animals which rise above the water. This region includes many animals that float on the surface and those who live near the surface.

2. The second picture is of the animals that more or less confine themselves to the first half mile of the ocean's surface. Sunlight penetrates much of this area, and its warm water teems with life. Most of the fish used for food and sport fishing live in this zone.

3. The third picture depicts the area between one-half mile to about two miles. Its waters are cold and dark. While some of the dwellers of this zone are large, many are small and strange looking. This zone is called the bathypelagic zone by oceanographers and marine biologists.

4. The bottom picture on the depth chart shows life below two miles. It is called the abyss. The pressure here is great, and the temperature of the water is near freezing. The only light comes from the luminescence of the creatures which dwell here. These creatures are generally small and grotesque.

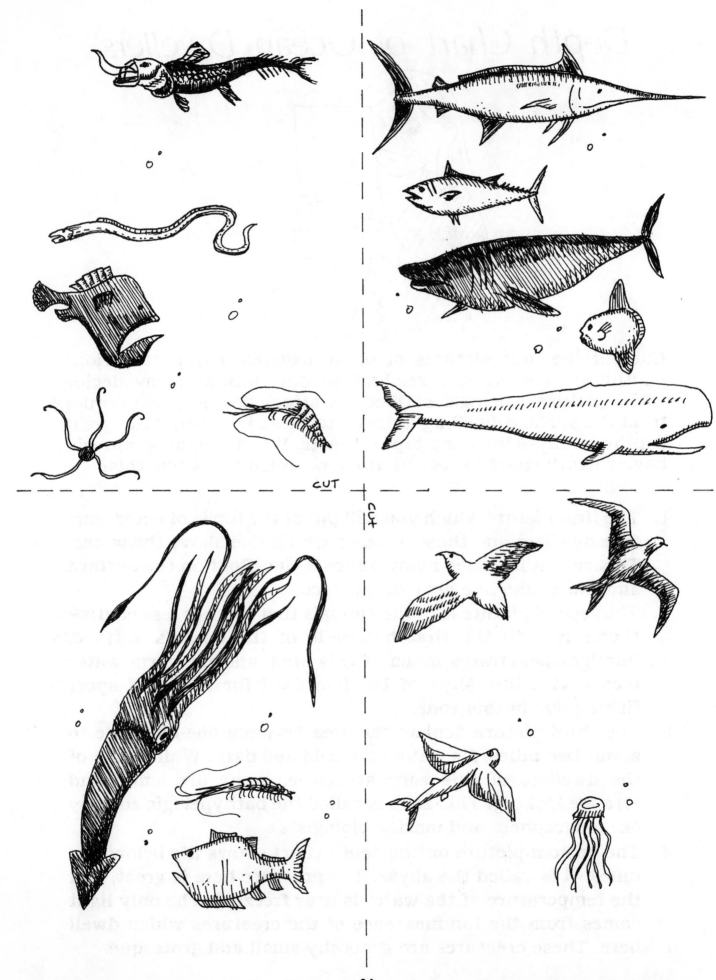

CUT

CUT

DRAWING WORDS OF MARINE ANIMALS

In drawing words, the purpose is to print the word in such a way as to show its meaning. Here are a few examples of drawing words associated with animals of the sea. Try drawing some words of your own which illustrate animals or plants of the sea.

SHARK-EXTERNAL FEATURES

Study the labeled drawing on the next page. From the description of the part fill in the name of the external feature of the shark.

1._____the five, sometimes seven, vertical openings on each side of the shark's body which allow water to pass over the gills.

2._____organ of sight.

3._____the first large fin located on the top of the shark's body.

4._____the first pair of fins located on the underside of the shark's body.

5._____the tail fin of the shark.

6._____the second pair of fins located on the underside of the shark.

7._____the indentation in the tail.

8._____a hole above the shark's eye which allows water to go directly to the gills.

9._____the second fin located on the topside of the shark's body.

10._____openings to the nasal passages.

11._____openings to the digestive tract.

12._____a protective membrane which covers the eye.

13._____the third set of fins on the underside of the body of a shark.

14._____a horizontal line of sensory cells which detects movement in the water.

After you have completed the above, describe the ways in which a shark's body is well equipped for life in the sea.

SHARK

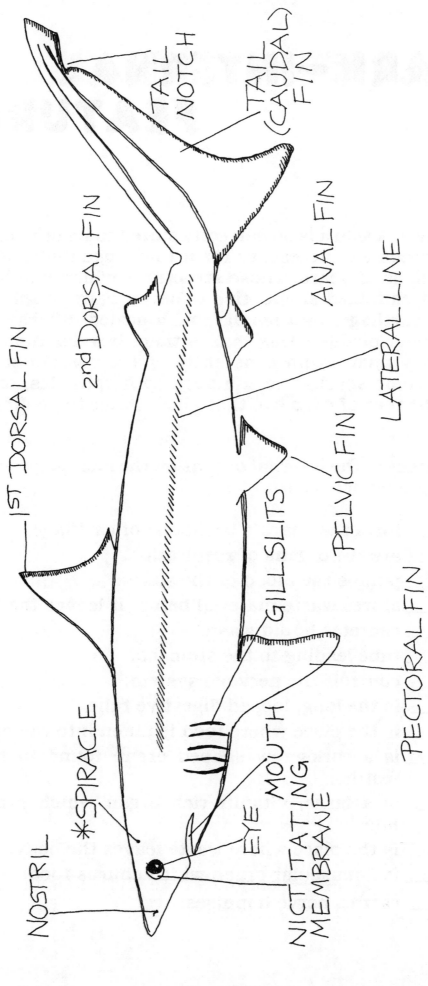

1ST DORSAL FIN

2nd DORSAL FIN

TAIL NOTCH

TAIL (CAUDAL) FIN

ANAL FIN

LATERAL LINE

PELVIC FIN

GILL SLITS

PECTORAL FIN

NOSTRIL

*SPIRACLE

EYE

MOUTH

NICTITATING MEMBRANE

*NOT FOUND IN ALL SHARKS

SHARK-INTERNAL FEATURES

The anatomy of a shark is so perfectly suited to its surroundings that it has become unnecessary for it to change its basic structure for millions of years. Those structures which readily identify it are streamlined shape, five to seven pairs of gill slits, a skeleton of cartilage, and small, rough scales. Sharks do not possess a swim bladder; this makes them heavier than water; therefore they must swim constantly or they would sink. For this reason some sharks are equipped with spiracles, or holes, located at the rear of each eye that allow water to go directly to the gills.

Match the names of the internal organs on the next page with the organ descriptions below.

1._____ form the shark's backbone of cartilage.
2._____ are the organs of respiration.
3._____ pumps the blood of the shark.
4._____ stores waste material before it leaves the body.
5._____ excretes liquid waste.
6._____ tube leading to the stomach.
7._____ controls the nervous system.
8._____ is the long, looped digestive tube.
9._____ is the place where food is taken into the body.
10._____ is a corkscrew-shaped organ found in the intestine.
11._____ is a large, vitamin-rich organ which produces bile.
12._____ is the place where waste leaves the body.
13._____ is a muscular organ which churns food.
14._____ carries nerve impulses.

SHARK INTERNAL

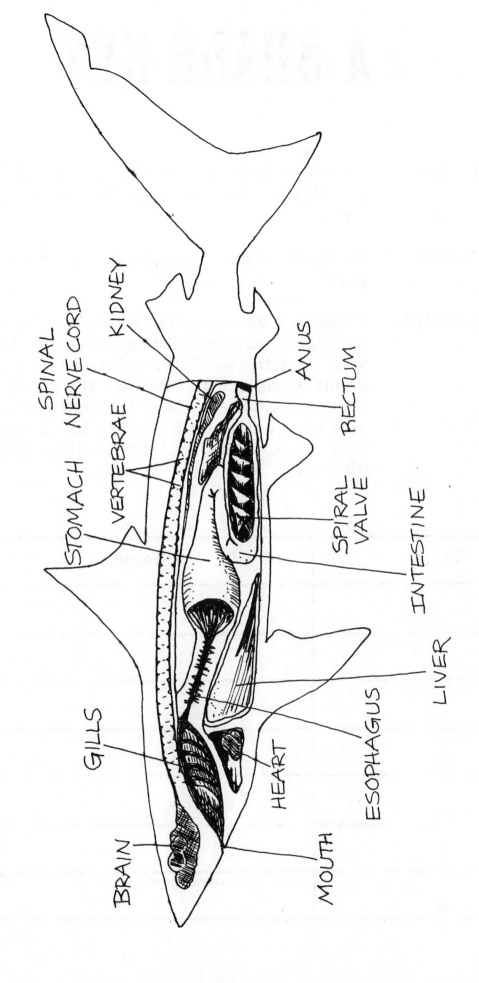

SPINAL
NERVE CORD
KIDNEY
VERTEBRAE
ANUS
RECTUM
STOMACH
SPIRAL VALVE
INTESTINE
GILLS
LIVER
HEART
ESOPHAGUS
BRAIN
MOUTH

A SHARK KEY

PURPOSE: To give students practice in using a key; to familiarize students with the characteristics of sharks.

MATERIALS: Pictures or drawings as provided on the next page.

PROCEDURE: A key is a valuable tool to anyone interested in the identification of living things. In using a key a student takes all the information he is given about an object and follows the given steps. In order to find the name of the shark, always start at 1A for each shark, determine if the description 1A or 1B fits, then follow the key as directed.

Shark	Name
a	
b	
c	
d	
e	
f	
g	

SHARK KEY

1A   Shark with first dorsal fin located midway between the pelvic fins and pectoral fins . . . . Great Blue Shark

1B   Shark with first dorsal fin nearer to the pectoral fins than to the pelvic fins or below pelvic fins . . . . See 2

2A   Shark with top shaded, giving striped effect . . Tiger Shark

2B   Shark with top having no striped effect . . . . See 3

3A   Shark with no unusual features such as elongated tail, flat head, or flat body . . . . See 5

3B   Shark with unusual features of the head, tail, or body . .See 4

4A   Shark with length of tail as long as the length of body . . . .
. . . . .Thresher Shark

4B   Unusual shark with tail within normal range . . . . See 6

5A   Slender shark with dorsal fin located almost above pectoral fins . . . . Mako

5B   Round-bodied shark with dorsal fin located almost above pectoral fins . . . . Mackerel Shark

6A   Shark with a normal-sized tail, but having flat, enlarged fins and a flat body . . . . Angel Shark

6B   Shark with a normal-sized tail and body, but having an unusual shaped head . . . . Hammerhead Shark

WHAT CREATURE IS THIS?

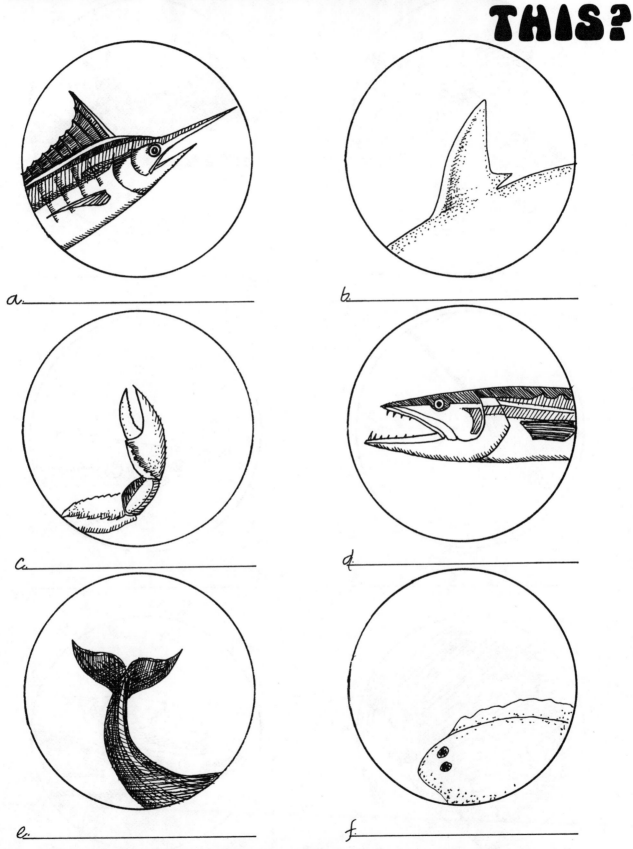

a. _____

b. _____

c. _____

d. _____

e. _____

f. _____

Can you identify the following oceanic creatures by seeing only a portion of their bodies? Be alert! They are not all fish.

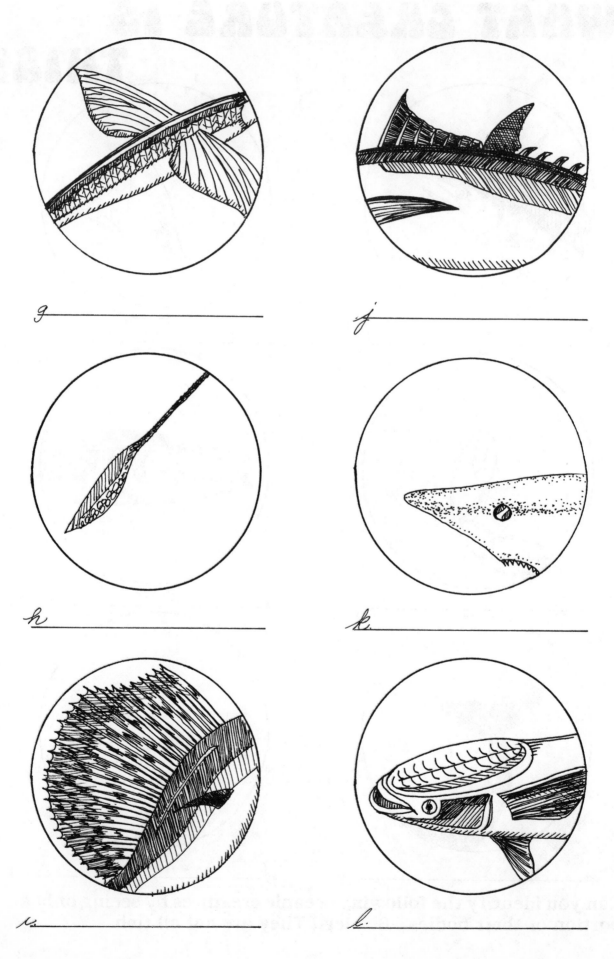

g _____

j _____

h _____

k. _____

k _____

l. _____

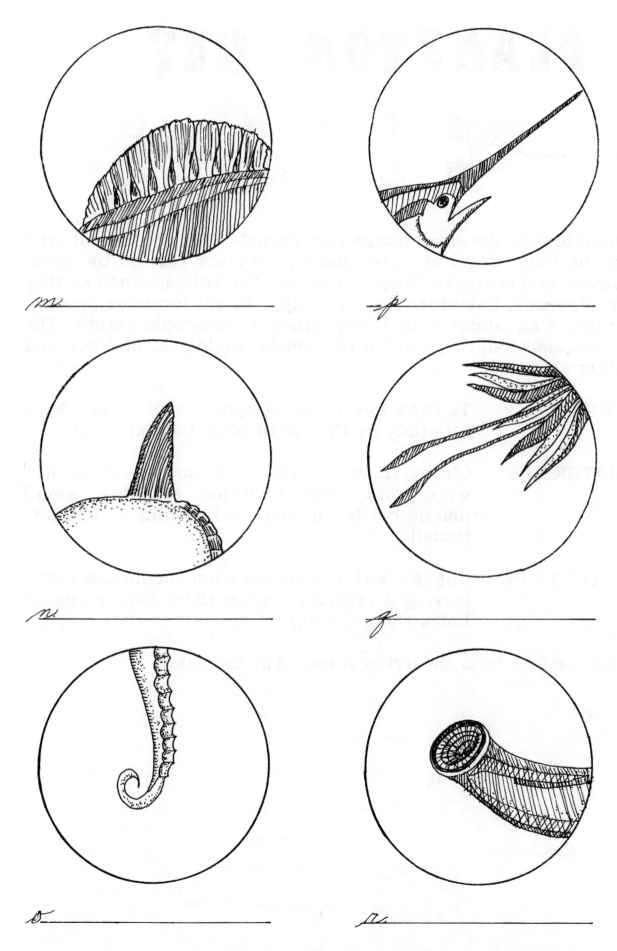

m. _____

p. _____

n. _____

q. _____

o. _____

r. _____

45

PLANKTON NET

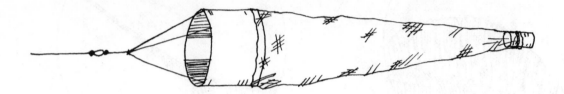

Plankton are the small plants and animals which swim and drift in the upper level of ocean water; they are carried by wind, waves, and currents. Zooplankton are the animals such as tiny crustaceans, immature fish, fish eggs, larval forms or oysters, crabs, etc., along with many other microscopic forms. The phytoplankton, or plant forms, consist mainly of diatoms and other algae.

PURPOSE: To show how oceanographers capture plankton for study by the use of plankton nets.

MATERIALS: Clean, rinsed bottle from household bleach, waterproof cement, nylon stocking, small plastic bottle, fishing cord, fishing swivel (optional).

PROCEDURE: Cut the bottom and top from the bleach bottle leaving a cylinder. Punch three evenly spaced holes along the top.

Cut the foot from the nylon stocking at the ankle.

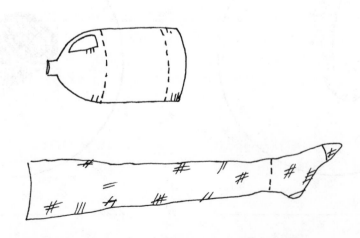

Glue the top of the stocking to the bottom of the cylinder.

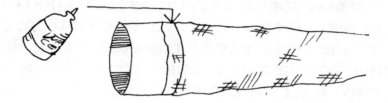

Secure the plastic bottle to the ankle part of the stocking by means of cord or rubber bands.

Attach fishing line to the top of the cylinder. A fishing swivel can be added for flexibility.

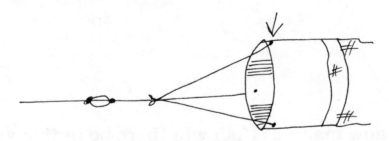

Your plankton net can be dragged in the ocean, a river, lake, or fast moving stream. The stocking will strain the organisms into the bottle. Transfer material from the collecting bottle into another container. Use a microscope to study the material you collect.

VARIATION: A coat hanger fashioned into a hoop can be substituted for the bleach bottle. Sew top of stocking around the coat hanger.

OCEANS OF CODFISH

A female codfish may spawn as many as 9,000,000 eggs annually. It takes five years for the eggs to develop into mature adults. At this time the life cycle may be repeated. Using this information, determine how many codfish could develop from the original pair only, if all were to survive.

1. If all survive, how many codfish will there be in five years?
   _____

2. In nature this does not actually happen. What prevents this from occurring? _____
   _____

3. If the codfish population stays the same (stabilizes), how many of the 9,000,000 eggs usually reach maturity? _____

4. Is the fact that all the codfish do not survive a good thing? Why? _____
   _____

WHALES

In general, there are two kinds of whales; one kind is toothless, the other is toothed. The toothless whales have baleen, or whalebone, which hangs from their upper jaws and is used as a strainer in obtaining large masses of small, shrimp-like animals known as krill. The belly of a baleen whale is pleated. This allows the jaw to hang open to scoop up seawater and all it contains. The baleen whale then closes its mouth and with its tongue forces the water out through the baleen leaving the krill, which it will swallow. The stomach of a baleen whale may contain as much as three tons of food. The blue whale, largest of all animals, is a baleen whale.

Toothed whales, such as the sperm whale, are also very large. They feed mainly on fish and squid. They are excellent divers and have been known to dive 3,000 feet and stay below the surface for as long as 90 minutes. A favorite food of the sperm whale is the giant squid. One can only imagine the ferocious, to-the-death battles which take place between these two creatures of the deep. Sperm whales have been caught with huge circular scars, the result of encounters with the powerful suckers on the arms of the giant squid.

Unlike humans, both kinds of baby whales are born tail first so that they may not drown. They are soon guided to the surface where their first contact with air stimulates breathing on their own. Their mothers supply them with a rich milk that is almost 50% fat. This milk provides the nutrients necessary for rapid growth and the formation of blubber to keep them warm when they return to cold waters.

WHALES

Using the information you have been given, tell whether the following descriptions apply to a toothless (baleen), a toothed, or both kinds of whales. Use the terms toothless, toothed or both.

1. _____ whales have flukes present.
2. _____ whales have small eyes.
3. _____ whales have mouths on topside of the heads.
4. _____ whales have mouths on bottom of the heads.
5. _____ whales have teeth present.
6. _____ whales have no teeth.
7. _____ whales have small side flippers present.
8. _____ whales eat krill.
9. _____ whales eat fish and squid.
10. _____ whales are mammals.
11. _____ whales have pleated bellies.
12. _____ whales have smooth bellies.

CINQUAIN OF THE SEA

A cinquain (sing'-kan) is a special kind of poem. The word cinquain comes from the French word *cinq*, which means five. The following poem is a cinquain:

Fish
Silvery white
Swimming, darting, rising
Silent in their world
Arrows.

Cinquains have five lines with a definite number of words and rules for each line. The first line is one word, the title. The second line is two words that describe the title. The third line is three words, expressing action. The fourth line is four words, describing a feeling. The last line is one word which could be used as the title.

Using plants, animals, or objects that are related in some way to the sea, compose a cinquain of your own in the space below.

_____

_____ _____

_____ _____ _____

_____ _ _____ _ _____

_____ .

VARIATION: Try reading your cinquain backwards.

Real or Imaginary?

Below are six exotic animals associated with the sea. Have all of them existed at some point in time or are some of them mythological or imaginary? Indicate by circling your choice.

1. Narwhal
   Real or imaginary?

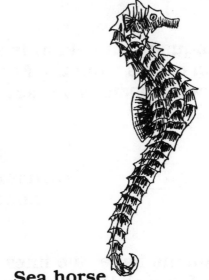

4. Sea horse
   Real or imaginary?

2. Dugong
   Real or imaginary?

5. Anglerfish
   Real or imaginary?

3. Mermaid
   Real or imaginary?

6. Convict fish
   Real or imaginary?

Records of the Sea

Below are some records of the sea. Some are animal records; others are records of places. How many of them do you know? Select your answers to the sea questions from the records.

1. _____ is considered the fastest fish.
2. _____ is the most venomous snake.
3. _____ is the largest mammal.
4. _____ probably produces the most valuable fur.
5. _____ is the largest ocean.
6. _____ is the deepest part of any of the oceans.
7. _____ lays the largest egg of any living animal.
8. _____ has the largest eyes.
9. _____ possesses the heaviest brain of all living animals.
10. _____ is the longest of all animals, stretched tip to tip.
11. _____ is the place where the tides are greatest.
12. _____ is the largest of all fish.
13. _____ is the saltiest body of water.
14. _____ are the largest waves.

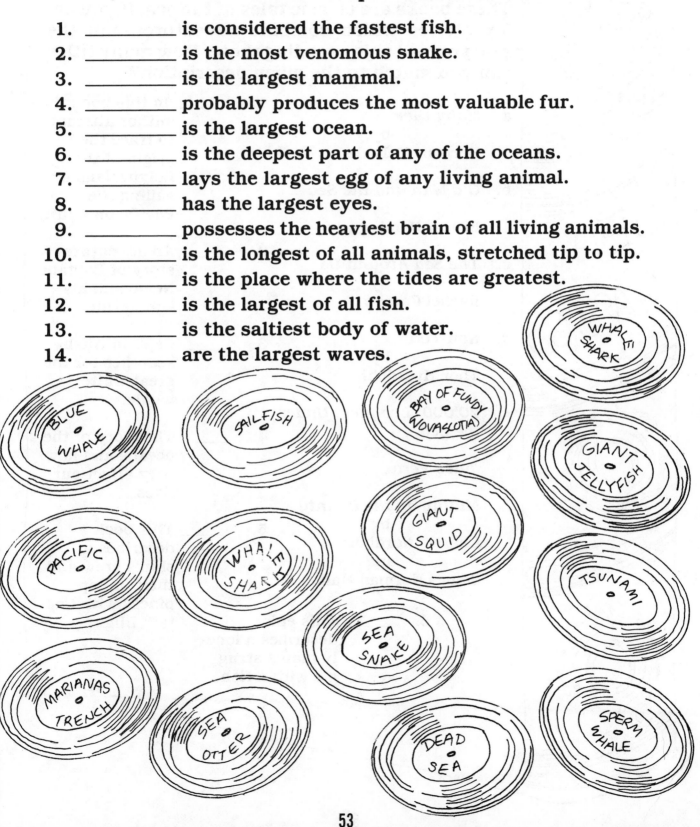

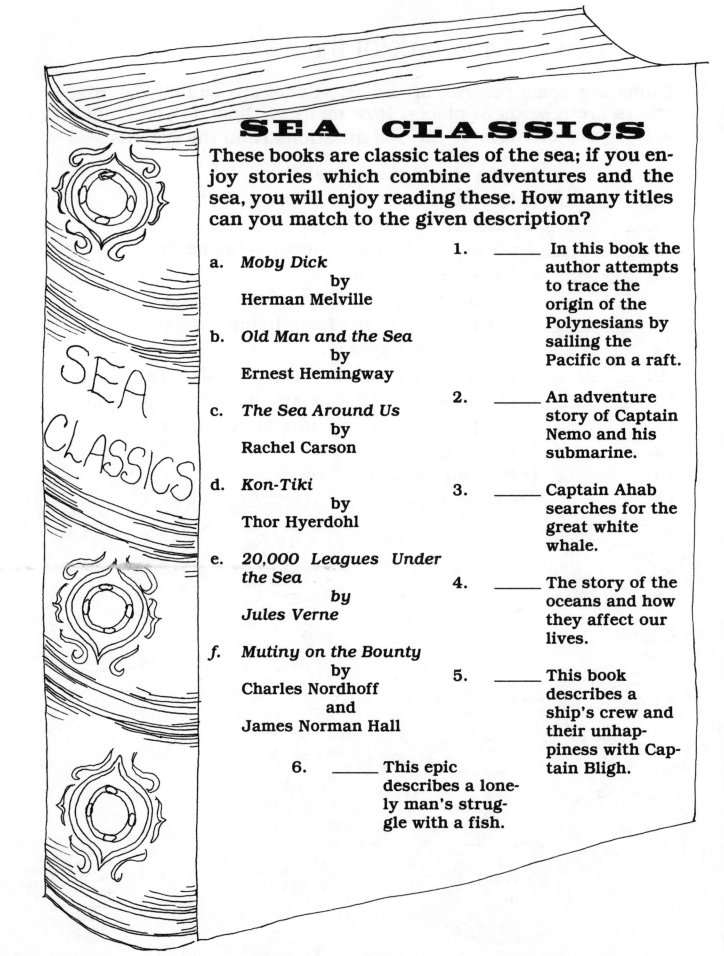

SEA CLASSICS

These books are classic tales of the sea; if you enjoy stories which combine adventures and the sea, you will enjoy reading these. How many titles can you match to the given description?

a. *Moby Dick*
by
Herman Melville

b. *Old Man and the Sea*
by
Ernest Hemingway

c. *The Sea Around Us*
by
Rachel Carson

d. *Kon-Tiki*
by
Thor Hyerdohl

e. *20,000 Leagues Under the Sea*
by
Jules Verne

f. *Mutiny on the Bounty*
by
Charles Nordhoff
and
James Norman Hall

1. _____ In this book the author attempts to trace the origin of the Polynesians by sailing the Pacific on a raft.

2. _____ An adventure story of Captain Nemo and his submarine.

3. _____ Captain Ahab searches for the great white whale.

4. _____ The story of the oceans and how they affect our lives.

5. _____ This book describes a ship's crew and their unhappiness with Captain Bligh.

6. _____ This epic describes a lonely man's struggle with a fish.

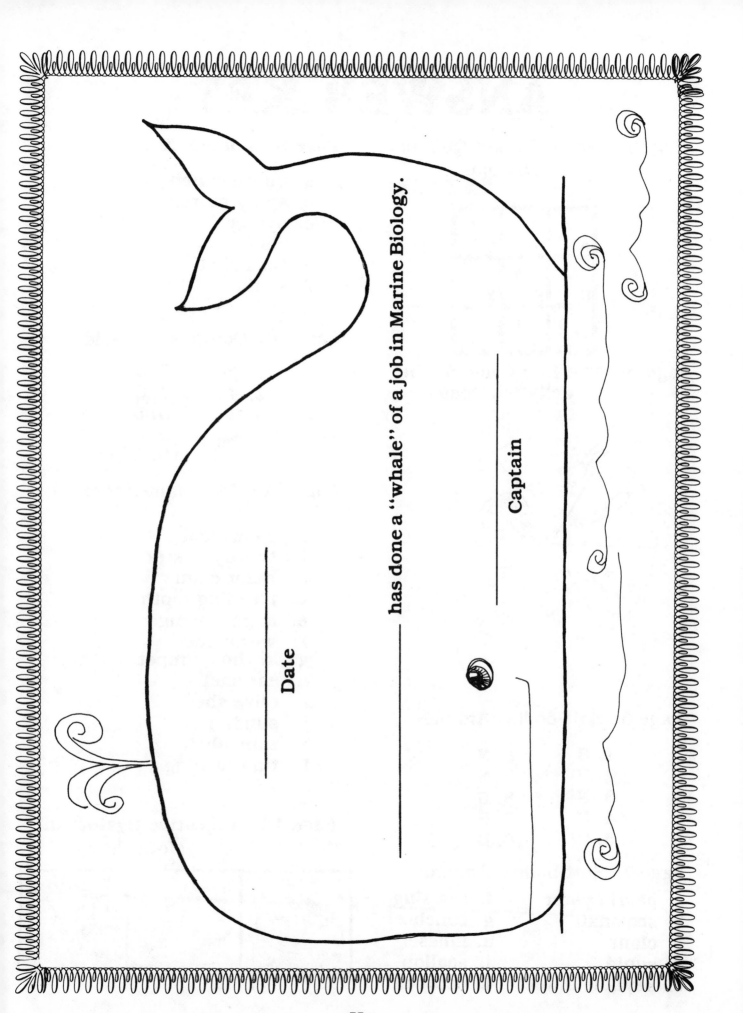

has done a "whale" of a job in Marine Biology.

Date

Captain

ANSWER KEY

Page 2: Magic Square Quiz on Diatoms

4 A	9 B	2 C
3 D	5 E	7 F
8 G	1 H	6 I

Page 5: The Life Cycle of the Jellyfish Obelia

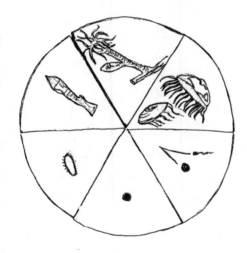

Page 6: Soft-bodied Animals

1. B   6. N
2. U   7. N
3. N   8. B
4. U   9. B
5. U   10. B

Page 7: Soft-bodied Animals

a. pearl oyster   f. sea slug
b. sea snail   g. conch
c. clam   h. mussel
d. squid   i. scallop
e. keyhole limpet   j. octopus

Page 8: Mollusk Key

a. queen conch
b. spiny murex
c. oyster
d. clam
e. tusk shell
f. squid
g. octopus

Page 10: Octopus or Squid?

1. O   6. S
2. S   7. O
3. B   8. B
4. S   9. B
5. O   10. B

Pages 11-12: Names that Fit

a. cone shell
b. thorny oyster
c. razor clam
d. bleeding tooth
e. angel's wings
f. worm shell
g. keyhole limpet
h. ear shell
i. olive shell
j. sundial
k. tulip shell
l. turkey wing

Page 13: Digestive System in Mollusks

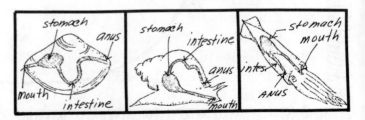

Page 13: (**cont'd.**)

Mouth takes in food.

Stomach aids in digestion.

Intestine digests and absorbs food.

Anus is the opening through which wastes are excreted.

Page 15: Clam (drawing)

1. mouth
2. anterior (front) adductor muscle
3. mantle
4. gonad (reproductive organ)
5. intestine
6. foot
7. incurrent (ingoing) siphon
8. excurrent (outgoing) siphon
9. anus
10. posterior (back) adductor muscle

Page 18: The Oyster Mystery

Solution: Starfish are able to regenerate into complete organisms from portions of the arms and centers; chopping them and returning the pieces to the ocean only served to increase the starfish population.

Page 20: Misnomers of the Sea

1. Jellyfish are not fish and they are not made of jelly.
2. A sea horse is not a horse; it is a fish.
3. Starfish are not fish; they are "star" shaped, spiny-skinned animals.
4. Sea cucumbers are not plants; they are spiny-skinned animals.
5. Shellfish are not fish.
6. A sea lily is not a plant; it is a spiny-skinned animal.
7. Sea cows are mammals; but they are not cows.
8. Dogfish are sharks.
9. Sea biscuits are spiny-skinned animals.
10. Sea feathers are spiny-skinned animals.
11. Horseshoe crabs are not crabs; they are related to spiders.
12. Sea robins are not birds; they are fish.

Page 22: Echinodermata

a. starfish
b. brittle star or serpent star
c. sea cucumber
d. sea urchin
e. sea lily

Page 24: Starfish

1. Echinodermata
2. Spiny-skinned
3. Orange, pink, red, green, blue, purple and brown
4. Center of the underside of the body
5. Walking and prying open the shells of mollusks
6. Eyespots
7. Sensitive to light and also to detect changes in the environment
8. Over 1700
9. Mollusks such as clams and oysters
10. Regulating the pressure in the tube feet
11. Simple
12. At the seashore, in the ocean; they are all marine.

Page 25: Starfish

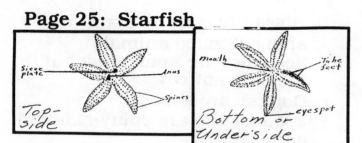

Page 26: Where Do Fish Get Oxygen?

1. Oxygen supports burning.
2. The Elodea produced the oxygen.
3. The pressure of the gas produced by the Elodea forced water out of the test tube.
4. Oceanic plants supply the oxygen for the oceanic animals.

Page 28: A Little Ecosystem of Your Own

1. The fish gives carbon dioxide and wastes to the ecosystem; it takes oxygen and food in the form of algae and microorganisms.
   The snail gives carbon dioxide and waste. It feeds on the decaying organic material and algae and uses oxygen supplied by the plants.
   The plants give oxygen and use the carbon dioxide supplied by the fish and snail. The wastes of the fish and snail fertilize the plants and promote the growth of algae (also plants).
2. This allows the chlorine to evaporate.
3. No. The plants need the light for photosynthesis.
4. Some or all of the plants and animals will die.

Page 31: Respiration Rate of Goldfish

1 - 3. Answers will vary.
4. Probably A. Fish can withstand cold better than heat.
5. Probably not. Heat would kill the cells.
6. Too much of a shock could be the result of adding the variable all at one time.
7. Amount of oxygen in water. Age and condition of the fish.
8. Answers will vary.

Page 32: Spelling Names of Fish

1. skate and flounder
2. toadfish, pipefish, herring, sunfish, haddock, sailfish, bluefish, swordfish, needlefish, sea horse.
3. toadfish, pipefish, sunfish, sailfish, bluefish, swordfish, needlefish, sea horse.
4. sole

Page 34: Depth Chart of Ocean Dwellers

1.
Bottom right

2.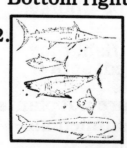
Upper right

3.
Lower left

4.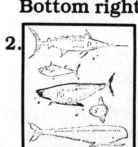
Upper left

Page 36:   Shark - External Features

1. Gill slits
2. Eye
3. 1st dorsal fin
4. Pectoral
5. Caudal
6. Pelvic
7. Caudal notch
8. Spiracle
9. 2nd dorsal fin
10. Nostrils
11. Mouth
12. Nictitating membrane
13. Anal fins
14. Lateral line

Page 38: Shark - Internal Features

1. Vertebrae
2. Gills
3. Heart
4. Rectum
5. Kidney
6. Esophagus
7. Brain
8. Intestine
9. Mouth
10. Spiral valve
11. Liver
12. Anus
13. Stomach
14. Spinal nerve cord

Page 40: Shark Key

a. Thresher
b. Mako
c. Mackerel
d. Hammerhead
e. Great Blue
f. Tiger
g. Angel

Page 43:   What Creature Is This?

a. head of a blue marlin
b. dorsal fin of a shark
c. claw of a crab
d. head of a barracuda
e. fluke of a whale
f. head of a flounder

Page 44:   What Creature Is This?

g. pectoral fins of a flying fish
h. tentacle of a squid
i. dorsal fin of a sailfish
j. dorsal fins of a tuna
k. head of a shark
l. remora with suckers on head

Page 45:   What Creature Is This?

m. top of a Portuguese man-o-war
n. dorsal fin of an ocean sun-fish
o. sea horse tail
p. swordfish head
q. arms of a squid
r. mouth of a lamprey eel

Page 48: Oceans of Codfish

1. 45,000,000. These are offspring from the original pair.
2. Some eggs are never fertilized, others are eaten, and the fish are eaten by other fish and animals, including man.
3. 2 or 3 maintain the population at an even number.
4. Yes, the ocean would be full of codfish.

Page 50: Whales

1. both
2. both
3. toothless
4. toothed
5. toothed
6. toothless
7. both
8. toothless
9. toothed
10. both
11. toothless
12. toothed

Page 52: Real or Imaginary?

1. Narwhal is real.
2. Dugong is real.
3. Mermaid is imaginary.

Page 52: (cont'd.)
4. Sea horse is real.
5. Anglerfish is real.
6. Convict fish is real.

Page 53: Records of the Sea
1. Sailfish
2. Sea snake
3. Blue whale
4. Sea otter
5. Pacific
6. Marianas trench
7. Whale shark
8. Giant squid
9. Sperm whale
10. Giant jellyfish
11. Bay of Fundy, Nova Scotia
12. Whale shark
13. Dead Sea
14. Tsunami

Page 54: Sea Classics
1. d
2. e
3. a
4. c
5. f
6. b